Creating Your USPs

Puts You

In Front of the (job) Pack!

©2012 Lulu Author. All rights reserved.
ISBN: 978-1-300-02254-1

Table of Contents

Introduction	1
Continuous Lifetime Improvement Process (CLIP) Self-Assessments	2-5
Strengths and Weakness Balance Sheet	3
Develop your strategic plan	3
Likes / Dislikes Survey	4
Achievements and Disappointments	5
Your USPs	6-12
Acquire New Skills	6
Identify Portable Skills	7-12
When Writing Your Résumé,	13-18
7 Steps to realization	
Cover letter – still *de rigueur*?	19
Expand Your Job Search Opportunities	20-23
Create your Network…Sources of Information	
Prevent Faux-Pas	24-35
Traditional versus Behavioral Interview Questions	
Make A Lasting Impression	36-39
Prepare Yourself For The Interview Day	36
The Pre-Interview Process	37
The Art of the Interview	38-39
Post-interview	40-41
SKYPE Interviews	42
Visual Self –Assessment	43-44
Underscore your USPs!	
Assess your performance	

Marketing Yourself
Creating your USPs (Unique Selling Points)

Whether the economy is up or down or whether this is your first time or your fifth time, job searches are stressful! Key core skills and expectations of employers, large or small, are worldwide to all career fields. Management luminary Tom Peters promoted the idea of self-marketing and his words still echo after 14 years. Peters wrote: "Regardless of age, regardless of position, regardless of the business we happen to be in, all of us need to understand the importance of branding. We are CEOs of our own companies: Me Inc."

***USP:** Product's differentiating characteristic. A characteristic of a product that makes it different from all similar products.*

A step-by-step instructional guide will pilot the reader to develop an unbeatable individual strategy. The self-assessing-exercise-driven handbook covers the gamut of job search preparation activities. Tasks include creating a portfolio of skills that can be applied in all areas; writing and fine-tuning résumés for "this job"; expanding job search opportunities – local, domestic, or international; making a lasting impression - 20 common interview questions and how to respond with confidence, interview do and don'ts, and post-interview follow up.

This guide will provide the reader with a toolkit to understand basic business needs and tailor the job search plan to exceed them!

Continuous Lifetime Improvement Process (CLIP)
Self-Assessments

USP: *Product's differentiating characteristic. A characteristic of a product that makes it different from all similar products*

☞ Conduct a self-assessment that identifies your skills.
- Build on your core skills
- Identify your key core skills
- Start a parallel career
- Make internal transition- you may move into a new area or be promoted
- Volunteer to take on what others don't want

Self-assessment
Learning about you is a Continuous Lifetime (of) Improvement Process. There are three (3) useful self-understanding tools:
1. Strengths and Weakness Balance Sheet
2. Likes / Dislikes Survey
3. Achievements and Disappointments

BE HONEST WITH YOURSELF!

① STRENGTHS *Maximum advantage* *Make your list*	WEAKNESSES *Avoid over-utilizing weaker qualities and skills*

Continuous Lifetime Improvement Process (CLIP)
Self-Assessments

Strategic Planning

definition: The process by which top management determines overall organizational purposes and objectives and how they are to be achieved. The ultimate outcome of the planning process will be recommended actions that implement strategy.

☞ **Develop Your Personal Strategic Plan**

- What skills would I need to do to diminish/eliminate my weaknesses?

- What are the skills I need to enhance my strengths?

- How do I go about getting these needed skills? (actions to implement your strategy)

Continuous Lifetime Improvement Process (CLIP)
Self-Assessments

② LIKES

| **DISLIKES** |
Helps one recognize the limitations we put on ourselves

Continuous Lifetime Improvement Process (CLIP)
Self-Assessments

③ ACHIEVEMENTS	Did I have support?

DISAPPOINTMENTS	What did I learn? *(Continuously improving)*

Continuous Lifetime Improvement Process (CLIP)
Self-Assessments

Integrating Business Needs With Your Value Added Skills

Business is looking for the following characteristics in their new hires. ✓ those that apply to you.
- ☐ drive
- ☐ enthusiastic
- ☐ innovative
- ☐ quick learners
- ☐ independent thinkers
- ☐ open minded
- ☐ know their way around a computer
- ☐ work well as part of a group
- ☐ have strong organization skills
- ☐ respectful of other cultures
- ☐ must be multi-culturally aware

To Acquire New Skills

- ⊕ to the conference you attend, add a session you know nothing about
- ⊕ seek out diverse friends; cultivate a circle of friends from all avenues of life
- ⊕ cross-pollinate ideas
- ⊕ know how to work cross-organizationally (up, down, across)
- ⊕ talk to people who are currently satisfied with their job
- ⊕ develop a data-gathering check sheet to identify some questions that need to be asked.

Continuous Lifetime Improvement Process (CLIP)
Self-Assessments

Identify Portable Skills
Instructions: *review the inventory of skills listed below. Checkmark those you do well. Add to list.*

E=Excellent   **S**=Strong   **A**=Able to

SKILL	E	S	A	SKILL	E	S	A
analytical skills				risk management			
bi-/multi-lingual skills				team building			
communication verbal/ written				telephone technique			
computer literate with spreadsheet				train and write user documentation			
computer skills				transfer responsibilities			
consensus builder skills				troubleshooting			
creative skills				work independently			
customer service skills				word processing skills			
decision making skills							
develop and document courses				YOU			
general management skills				are a problem solver			
interpersonal skills				are results-oriented			
leadership skills				have courage to change things			
marketing skills				like task diversity			
meet multiple deadlines				key skill: Innovate			
motivate others				possess a great sense of urgency			
motivation skills				are FLEXIBLE!			
project management skills							
promotional skills (promoting causes / people)							

Flexibility means	THE OBJECTIVE:
✦ rebounding after being downsized ✦ being adaptable enough to do all the work required of a skeletal Staff ✦ smart enough and secure enough to make a lateral move ✦ willing to go where ever the jobs are ✦ WELCOME re-education!	To possess a portfolio of USPs (skills) you can apply in many areas. **SOLUTION** ✦ You must be **multi-task** oriented

Continuous Lifetime Improvement Process (CLIP)
Self-Assessments

☞ **Identify Portable Skills**

EDUCATION

High School / Subjects	*Are there topics you would pursue now?*

College(s)	

Continuous Lifetime Improvement Process (CLIP)
Self-Assessments

☞ **Identify Portable Skills**

CEU(S)	

Summer Jobs	*Is there a summer job that you enjoyed and may want to pursue?*

Continuous Lifetime Improvement Process (CLIP)
Self-Assessments

☞ **Identify Portable Skills**

PROFESSIONAL ORGANIZATIONS	*What skills did you learn?*

Continuous Lifetime Improvement Process (CLIP)
Self-Assessments

☞ **Identify Portable Skills**

CIVIC / COMMUNITY AFFILIATIONS	*What skills did you learn?*

Continuous Lifetime Improvement Process (CLIP)
Self-Assessments

RATE YOUR WORK VALUES
Prioritize from 1-7
(1 = best)

☐ Income

☐ Independence

☐ Security

☐ Leadership

☐ Prestige

☐ Helping Others

☐ Outside Activities

DEFINE YOUR WORK INTEREST(S)

Industry	Geographic Location
Public Private	*Local:*
BE MORE SPECIFIC Public, Private,	Relocate: DOMESTIC State _____ Area _____
and (still) MORE SPECIFIC	Relocate: INTERNATIONAL Country _____ Area _____

Example:
Be more specific
- *Public, health care*
- *Private, pharmaceutical*

And (still) more specific
- *Johnson & Johnson*
- *Glaxco*

- Research the industry to familiarize yourself with what the company is doing.

- Research your destination to find out more about the area you wish to live in.

WHEN WRITING YOUR RÉSUMÉ,

♪ Things to remember:

- Write multiple résumés to fit the industry, job and role you are applying for. For each, enumerate the reasons the company should hire you.
- Stay current. Old school résumés focus on duties performed. New-school résumés focus on bottom-line results.
- Know the competition pool and highlight education or employment accordingly. Critical components should be captured within a 20-to-30 second screening window.
- Error-free! You only have one shot to make a good impression.
- Use powerful words that communicate action.
- Highlight ROI you achieved for previous employers. Be specific.
- Length? Students and entry-level job seekers – one page; Top executives and professionals – use as many pages as needed.

1. Remember your **target audience** (what can this person do for our organization). Target your résumé to the position you want.

2. List your **contact information** first at the top of the résumé - your name, address, phone number and e-mail address - so you can be contacted.

3. Present **education** in reverse chronological order - graduate and undergraduate education, and names, locations and dates. *(reference CLIP exercise, page 8 & 9)*

When Writing Your Résumé,

4. **Experience**
   - Choose the appropriate format. Chronological, functional or combination of both.
   - Reverse chronological order, your *past and present job*. List employer, location and dates (years)
   - *Outline major accomplishments and summarize* what you achieved in each position that contributed to the organization's goals.
     - Be brief and precise.
     - Begin each sentence with an action verb.
     - Document accomplishments.

Name　　　　　　　Tele. # Address　　　　　e-mail address: **Value-Added Statement** (intro – USP) **Education** **Experience** **Personal/other**	Name　　　　　　　Tele. # Address　　　　　e-mail address: **Value-Added Statement** (intro – USP) **Experience** **Education** **Personal/other**

First résumé

exercise:
Identify powerful action verbs:

outlined	calculated		
increased	produced		
enhanced	secured		

When Writing Your Résumé,

4. Experience

When Writing Your Résumé,

5. Additional (if applicable) sections

Athletics

Certifications

Community Activities

Languages

When Writing Your Résumé,

5. Additional (if applicable) sections

| **Professional Affiliations** |
| |

| **Publications** |
| |

| **Special Interests** |
| |

| **Travel** |
| |

When Writing Your Résumé,

6. **Added-value statement, mission statement, objective**
   - What attributes do you have that will add value to the organization? Remember to identify your unique selling point(s)! Use the space below to brainstorm.

   ♪ *USP: Product's differentiating characteristic. A characteristic of a product that makes it different from all similar products*

   - Place after Contact information and Experience/Education Section.
     - Many find it easier to write after compiling résumé.

7. **References**
   a. Select based on the requirements of the job.
      1. Can they contribute to establishing areas of your expertise?
   b. Ask references before compiling your list. *(common courtesy, professional)*
   c. Let them know the specifics of the job you want so they are prepared to tailor their responses accordingly.
   d. Make sure all reference data is accurate to facilitate contact.

Contact name	Job title	Phone/cell #	e-mail address	Company Name	Address	✓

COVER LETTER
Still de rigueur?

- If requested, include.
- Be concise. Match posted position's job requirements with your qualifications.
- Quantify achievements.
- Use bullet-points to reduce "read" time and increase "impact" time.
- To build a personal connection mention those you may know at the organization.

- If you do not need to send a cover letter, list a well-written summary of your qualifications at the top of your résumé. *(see pg. 18 – Your Value-added Statement)*

*✐ Remember: Focus on what **you** can do for the company, **not** what the company can do for you.*

EXPAND YOUR JOB SEARCH OPPORTUNITIES
Create your Network…Sources of Information

◈ **<u>Friends, Family</u>**

Name	address	e-mail address	tele/cellphone #	contacted

Expand Your Job Search Opportunities
Create your Network…Sources of Information

◈ Job / Career Fairs

Fair	Location	Date	Attended

◈ Employment agencies

Agency	Location	Date	Attended

◈ Professional Organizations

Organization	Contact Person / Website	✓

Expand Your Job Search Opportunities
Create your Network…Sources of Information

◈ Trade magazines

Magazine	Contact Person / Website	✓

◈ International Newspapers

Newspaper	Contact Person / Website	✓

◈ Television Media

Station	Contact Person / Website	✓

Expand Your Job Search Opportunities
Create your Network…Sources of Information

- **Internet / Social Media**

		✓

- **Chambers of Commerce listings - city / state / country specific**

	Contact Person / Website	✓

- Library

- Help-wanted Ads

- Telephone book (Business section / yellow pages)

- Annual reports

- Company newsletter

PREVENT *FAUX-PAS*
20 Common Interview Questions

- Before going into an interview, be ready for difficult questions.
  - In a **traditional interview**, you will be asked questions that solicit a straight-forward response – "What are your strengths and weaknesses?" *(determines how you **will** behave)*   *[see pg. 2, Strengths & Weaknesses]*
  - In a **behavioral interview**, you will be asked questions that solicit whether or not you have the skills required by the employer *(determines how you **did** behave)*. [see pg. 7- 11 – Identify Portable Skills]

- Answers should be 15 seconds to 1.5 minutes.
  - Answer questions and back up your statements with specific examples.
  - Ask for clarification if you don't understand a question.
  - Be thorough in your responses.
  - Be concise in your wording.

- Being prepared reduces your fears!

1.) Describe a time when you were faced with problems or stresses at work that tested your coping skills.	
2.) Give me an example of when you felt you were able to build motivation in your coworkers or associates.	

Prevent *Faux-Pas*
20 Common Interview Questions

3.) Give me an example of an important goal you had to set and tell me about your progress in reaching that goal.	
4.) Tell me about a time when you had to use your spoken communication skills and tell other people what you thought or felt.	

Prevent *Faux-Pas*
20 Common Interview Questions

5.) Give me an example of a time when you had to be relatively quick in coming to a decision.	
6.) Give me an example of a time when you were able to communicate successfully with another person, even when that individual may not have personally liked you.	

Prevent *Faux-Pas*
20 Common Interview Questions

7.) Describe the most creative work-related project you have completed.	
8.) Describe your most recent group effort.	

Prevent *Faux-Pas*
20 Common Interview Questions

9.) Tell me about a specific occasion when you conformed to a policy even though you did not agree with it.	
10.) Describe the most significant written document, report, or presentation that you've completed.	

Prevent *Faux-Pas*
20 Common Interview Questions

11.) Give me an example of a time when you had to go above and beyond the call of duty in order to get a job done.	
12.) What did you do in your last job in order to be effective with your organization and planning? Be specific.	

Prevent *Faux-Pas*
20 Common Interview Questions

13.) Describe the worst customer or coworker you have ever had and tell me how you dealt with him or her.	
14.) Describe a situation in which you were able to positively influence the actions of others in a desired direction.	

Prevent *Faux-Pas*
20 Common Interview Questions

15.) Tell me about a situation in the past year in which you had to deal with a very upset customer or coworker.	
16.) Describe a situation in which others within your organization depended on you.	

Prevent *Faux-Pas*
20 Common Interview Questions

17.) What did you do in your last job to contribute toward a teamwork environment? Be specific.	
18.) Describe a time when you felt it was necessary to modify or change your actions in order to respond to the needs of another person.	

Prevent *Faux-Pas*
20 Common Interview Questions

19.) Give me an example of a time when you used your fact-finding skills to gain information needed to solve a problem.	
20.) *(referencing #19)* Tell me how you analyzed the information and came to a decision.	

Prevent *Faux-Pas*

☞ Talk about your strengths (how will you fit in)
      Reminder: Review the skills checklist from pages 7-11.

ATTRIBUTES
define
- noun
- A quality, property, or characteristic of somebody or something

Synonyms:
- trait
- feature
- mannerism
- peculiarity

☑ ***Checkmark those that apply:***

☐ tenacious
☐ moral
☐ honest
☐ fair
☐ creative
☐ trustworthy
☐ authentic
☐ open
☐ curious
☐ big-picture
☐ considerate
☐ agile
☐ resilient

☐ growing
☐ generous
☐ other-minded
☐ contributing
☐ honest
☐ connecting
☐ adaptable
☐ determined
☐ compassionate
☐ focused
☐ kind
☐ courageous
☐ improving

Attributes
- What are your 5 best attributes [for ***this*** job]?

exercise

I am

1. *sample response*: **tenacious**	
2. *sample response*: **generous**	
3.	
4.	
5.	

Prevent *Faux-Pas*

exercise
- *Can you do what you say?*

I demonstrated my (# 1 - 5) when I

TIP:
(Designate the number of the *Faux-Pas* scenario that answers this statement).

1. *(tenacious)* <u>**Pioneered, piloted and proved a new customer response system and cut complaints by 87 percent.**</u> (7. Describe the most creative work-related project you have completed.)
2. *(generous)* <u>**Volunteered to mentor new hires before and after work hours and cut first 90-day turnover by 72 percent.**</u> (14. Describe a situation in which you were able to positively influence the actions of others in a desired direction.)
3.
4.
5.

◈ Specific achievements put you in front of the pack.

◈ Being able to respond to questions without hesitation says to the interviewer, "this person knows what they are talking about and can articulate it well" *(core skill)*.

35

MAKE A LASTING IMPRESSION
Prepare Yourself For The Interview Day

1.) Develop **Your** Interview Checklist ☑

☐ Does the company offer career guidance?

☐ How far can I go at this company? (as a woman, a minority, etc)

☐ Does this company encourage career development?

☐ Will the company allow me to balance my professional and personal needs?

☐ Is this company or division financially fit?

☐ Could I be happy here?

2.) Research the company *[see pg. 12– Define Your Work Interest]*
- Bring your notes about the company

3.) Arrive 15 minutes before
- Give yourself time to "exhale"

4.) Dress appropriately for the industry
- Impeccable personal grooming and hygiene

5.) Go alone
- Find a sitter for small children

6.) Take
- plenty of résumés and business cards
- quarters for parking meters
- extra pair of nylons, ladies
- a small portfolio of sample work (bring several copies just in case)

♦ Be nice to the receptionist when you walk in and walk out! (they may be asked for their opinion of you.)

The Pre-Interview Process

The Application Form

Remember to take all necessary information to complete the application form.
- ☐ driver's license
- ☐ passport
- ☐ green card
- ☐ shot records/medical
- ☐ list of references

- Complete the entire application
- Mark "N/A" where applicable
    - A blank may indicate you overlooked/missed it.

✏ **Remember,** *first impressions* ...   employers are looking to see if you have the three most basic communication skills:
1. Read and understand instructions
2. Spell correctly
3. Write in complete sentences

The Art of the Interview

- ✦ Offer a firm handshake.
- ✦ Make eye contact.
- ✦ Have a friendly expression when you are greeted by the interviewer.
- ✦ Listen to be sure you understand your interviewer's name and the correct pronunciation.
- ✦ Address your interviewer by title (Ms., Dr., Mr.) and last name, until invited to do otherwise.
- ✦ Be honest & be yourself.

- ✦ Speak clearly and concisely.
- ✦ Do not offer information.
- ✦ Ask questions. (*✏ remember your checklist*)
- ✦ Exhibit a positive attitude throughout the interview!
- ✦ Sit up straight!
- ✦ Let the interviewer know how to take your skills and apply.

The Art of the Interview

exercise:

☛ Pick 3 traits from your top 5 best attributes list (select the top 3 requirements for this job).

1.)
2.)
3.)

exercise:

☛ Be able to respond with **action** words

"I could put my (#1 - 3) to work for you by ... ."

1.)
2.)
3.)

sample: "I could put my ***attentiveness to detail*** to work for you by double checking the annual report each year."

 ☙ Communicating your strengths helps reduce the employer's fears of hiring you.

The Art of the Interview

Body Language

- Maintain good eye contact during the interview.
- Sit still in your seat; avoid fidgeting and slouching.
- Smile.

Interview Don'ts

- cross your arms, position your body sideways to the speaker or physically back away from the conversation. This can convey disagreement or lack of interest.
- chew gum.
- twirl / play with your hair.
- Rudeness is inexcusable! Don't
    - interrupt the speaker.
    - take a call on your cell-phone.
    - tweet.
- make excuses. Take responsibility for your actions.
- act as if you would take any job or are desperate for employment.
- exhibit frustration or a negative attitude.
- bad-mouth your previous employer(s).

Before leaving,

- Ask for an appropriate "follow up".
- Re-iterate your interest in the job.

Making A Lasting Impression

- ☑ Show confidence.
- ☑ Talk intelligently.
- ☑ Look presentable.
- ☑ BE PREPARED!

POST-INTERVIEW

☛ **Review Your Interview Checklist**   ☑ All that comply

☐ Does the company offer career guidance?
☐ How far can I go at this company? (as a woman, a minority, etc)

☐ Does this company encourage career development?
☐ Will the company allow me to balance my professional and personal needs?

☐ Is this company or division financially fit?
☐ Could I be happy here?

☛ **Evaluate Yourself**
- Immediately make a list of the things you did well and those things you feel you need to do better the next time.

☑ I did well …

Post-Interview

☞ **Evaluate Yourself**

☒ I need to improve…	HOW?

☞ **Follow Up**
- E-mail a thank you note within 24 hours to the company Human Resource person and any person you interviewed with.
- Send a handwritten thank-you note within 1-3 days after the interview.

SUMMARY
Your USPs will make you irresistible!

- Showcase your work (include a link to an online portfolio). Let them know your USP(s)!
- Learn as much about the company you will be interviewing with.
- Tailor your responses to company's needs.
- Demonstrate listening skills in the interview by paraphrasing what your interviewer has shared.
- Send a thank you note.
- Think POSITIVE!

SKYPE INTERVIEWS

Video interviewing is becoming more and more "the norm" in the current economic time. This provides the opportunity for you to showcase your USP by providing you with the ability to prepare a digital portfolio that can be used for the interview. Be prepared for your interview:

1.) Look directly at the video camera you are using.

2.) Eliminate interruptions.
• Turn off phones
• Let the family know the noise level must be zero. (move pets if necessary)

3.) As with any public presentation, practice first in front of a mirror. Self-evaluate your body language. Ask for feedback from friends and family who will be honest with you.

4.) Your surroundings
• Shoot your video against a blank or warm-colored background.
• Place awards and certificates behind you to showcase your achievements.

5.) Plan your clothing carefully – business-wear conveys your professionalism.

6.) Speak concisely and more quickly than you normally do.

7.) Portray yourself enthusiastically!

☞ Test your audio and video equipment to insure they are working properly!

VISUAL SELF–ASSESSMENT
Underscore your USPs!

- **USP:** *Product's differentiating characteristic. A characteristic of a product that makes it different from all similar products*

- Eliminate *fear* and gain confidence … Practice, Practice, Practice!

- Have a friend take you through a "mock" interview and tape it.

- Assess your **strengths**, your **weaknesses**.

Assess Your Performance

☑ I did well … 

Visual Self–Assessment
Underscore your USPs!

Assess Your Performance

	☒ I need to improve… 	HOW?

☹ HANDLING REJECTION

- Learning how to handle rejection in a positive way is a must!
- Do not let it bring you down.

- Show professionalism and graciousness by sending a thank you note. *("I appreciate the time you allowed me to interview with your organization.")* This will be remembered.
- Prepare for the next interview!

www.ingramcontent.com/pod-product-compliance
Lightning Source LLC
Chambersburg PA
CBHW081145170526
45158CB00009BA/2686